# Thrawn Janet

**Robert Louis Stevenson**

# Kessinger Publishing's Rare Reprints

## Thousands of Scarce and Hard-to-Find Books on These and other Subjects!

- Americana
- Ancient Mysteries
- Animals
- Anthropology
- Architecture
- Arts
- Astrology
- Bibliographies
- Biographies & Memoirs
- Body, Mind & Spirit
- Business & Investing
- Children & Young Adult
- Collectibles
- Comparative Religions
- Crafts & Hobbies
- Earth Sciences
- Education
- Ephemera
- Fiction
- Folklore
- Geography
- Health & Diet
- History
- Hobbies & Leisure
- Humor
- Illustrated Books
- Language & Culture
- Law
- Life Sciences

- Literature
- Medicine & Pharmacy
- Metaphysical
- Music
- Mystery & Crime
- Mythology
- Natural History
- Outdoor & Nature
- Philosophy
- Poetry
- Political Science
- Science
- Psychiatry & Psychology
- Reference
- Religion & Spiritualism
- Rhetoric
- Sacred Books
- Science Fiction
- Science & Technology
- Self-Help
- Social Sciences
- Symbolism
- Theatre & Drama
- Theology
- Travel & Explorations
- War & Military
- Women
- Yoga
- *Plus Much More!*

**We kindly invite you to view our catalog list at:**
**http://www.kessinger.net**

# THRAWN JANET

BY

ROBERT LOUIS STEVENSON

# THRAWN JANET

BY ROBERT LOUIS STEVENSON

THE REVEREND MURDOCH SOULIS
was long minister of the moorland parish of
Balweary, in the vale of Dule. A severe, bleak-
faced old man, dreadful to his hearers, he dwelt in
the last years of his life, without relative or servant
or any human company, in the small and lonely
manse under the Hanging Shaw. In spite of the
iron composure of his features, his eye was wild,
scared, and uncertain; and when he dwelt, in pri-
vate admonitions, on the future of the impenitent,
it seemed as if his eye pierced through the storms
of time to the terrors of eternity. Many young
persons, coming to prepare themselves against
the season of the holy communion, were dread-
fully affected by his talk. He had a sermon
on 1 Pet. v. 8, "The devil as a roaring lion,"
on the Sunday after every 17th of August, and
he was accustomed to surpass himself upon that
text both by the appalling nature of the matter
and the terror of his bearing in the pulpit. The
children were frightened into fits, and the old
looked more than usually oracular, and were, all
that day, full of those hints that Hamlet depre-

cated. The manse itself, where it stood by the water of Dule among some thick trees, with the Shaw overhanging it on the one side, and on the other many cold, moorish hilltops rising toward the sky, had begun, at a very early period of Mr. Soulis's ministry, to be avoided in the dusk hours by all who valued themselves upon their prudence; and guidmen sitting at the clachan alehouse shook their heads together at the thought of passing late by that uncanny neighbourhood. There was one spot, to be more particular, which was regarded with especial awe. The manse stood between the high-road and the water of Dule, with a gable to each; its back was toward the kirktown of Balweary, nearly half a mile away; in front of it, a bare garden, hedged with thorn, occupied the land between the river and the road. The house was two stories high, with two large rooms on each. It opened not directly on the garden, but on a causewayed path, or passage, giving on the road on the one hand, and closed on the other by the tall willows and elders that bordered on the stream. And it was this strip of causeway that enjoyed among the young parishioners of Balweary so infamous a reputation. The minister walked there often after dark, sometimes groaning aloud in the instancy of his unspoken prayers; and when he was from home, and the manse door was locked, the more daring school-boys ventured, with beating hearts, to "follow my leader" across that legendary spot. This atmosphere of terror, surrounding, as it did, a man of God of spotless character and orthodoxy, was a common cause of wonder and subject of inquiry among the few strangers who were led by chance or business into that unknown, outlying country. But many even of the people of the parish were ignorant of the strange events which had marked the first year of Mr. Soulis's ministrations; and among those who were better informed, some were naturally reticent, and others shy of that particular topic. Now and again, only, one of the older folk would warm into courage over his third tumbler, and recount the cause of the minister's strange looks and solitary life.

Fifty years syne, when Mr. Soulis cam' first into Ba'weary, he was still a young man,—a callant, the folk said,—fu' o' book-learnin' and grand at the exposition, but, as was natural in sae young a man, wi' nae leevin' experience in religion. The younger sort were greatly taken wi' his gifts and his gab; but auld, concerned, serious men and women were moved even to prayer for the young man, whom they took to be a self-deceiver, and the parish that was like to be sae ill supplied. It was before the days o' the Moderates—weary fa' them; but ill things are like guid—they baith come bit by bit, a pickle at a time; and there were folk even then that said the Lord had left the college professors to their ain devices, an' the lads that went to study wi' them wad hae done mair and better sittin' in a peat-bog, like their forebears of the persecution, wi'

a Bible under their oxter and a speerit o' prayer in
their heart. There was nae doubt, onyway, but that
Mr. Soulis had been ower-lang at the college. He
was careful and troubled for mony things besides
the ae thing needful. He had a feck o' books wi'
him—mair than had ever been seen before in a'
that presbytery; and a sair wark the carrier had
wi' them, for they were a' like to have smoored in
the Deil's Hag between this and Kilmackerlie.
They were books o' divinity, to be sure, or so they
ca'd them; but the serious were o' opinion there
was little service for sae mony, when the hail o'
God's Word would gang in the neuk of a plaid.
Then he wad sit half the day and half the nicht
forby, which was scant decent—writin', nae less;
and first they were feard he wad read his sermons; and syne it proved he was writin' a book
himsel', which was surely no fittin' for ane of his
years an' sma' experience.

Onyway, it behooved him to get an auld, decent
wife to keep the manse for him an' see to his bit
denners; and he was recommended to an auld
limmer,—Janet M'Clour, they ca'd her,—and sae
far left to himsel' as to be ower-persuaded. There
was mony advised him to the contrar', for Janet was
mair than suspeckit by the best folk in Ba'weary.
Lang or that, she had had a wean to a dragoon;
she hadnae come forrit [1] for maybe thretty year;
and bairns had seen her mumblin' to hersel' up on

---

[1] To "come forrit"—to offer one's self as a commu-
nicant.

Key's Loan in the gloamin', whilk was an unco
time an' place for a God-fearin' woman.   Howso-
ever, it was the laird himsel' that had first tauld the
minister o' Janet; and in thae days he wad have
gane a far gate to pleesure the laird.   When folk
tauld him that Janet was sib to the deil, it was a'
superstition by his way of it; an' when they cast
up the Bible to him, an' the witch of Endor, he
wad threep it doun their thrapples that thir days
were a' gane by, and the deil was mercifully re-
strained.

Weel, when it got about the clachan that Janet
M'Clour was to be servant at the manse, the folk
were fair mad wi' her an' him thegether; and some
o' the guidwives had nae better to dae than get
round her door-cheeks and chairge her wi' a' that
was kent again' her, frae the sodger's bairn to John
Tamson's twa kye.   She was nae great speaker;
folk usually let her gang her ain gait, an' she let
them gang theirs, wi' neither fair guid-e'en nor
fair guid-day; but when she buckled to, she had
a tongue to deave the miller.   Up she got, an'
there wasnae an auld story in Ba'weary but she
gart somebody lowp for it that day; they couldnae
say ae thing but she could say twa to it; till, at
the hinder end, the guidwives up and claught
haud of her, and clawed the coats aff her back,
and pu'd her doun the clachan to the water o'
Dule, to see if she were a witch or no, soum or
droun.   The carline skirled till ye could hear her
at the Hangin' Shaw, and she focht like ten; there

was mony a guid wife bure the mark of her neist day an' mony a lang day after; and just in the hettest o' the collieshangie, wha suld come up (for his sins) but the new minister.

"Women," said he (and he had a grand voice), "I charge you in the Lord's name to let her go."

Janet ran to him—she was fair wud wi' terror —an' clang to him, an' prayed him, for Christ's sake, save her frae the cummers; an' they, for their pairt, tauld him a' that was kent, and maybe mair.

"Woman," says he to Janet, "is this true?"

"As the Lord sees me," says she, "as the Lord made me, no a word o' 't. Forby the bairn," says she, "I 've been a decent woman a' my days."

"Will you," says Mr. Soulis, "in the name of God, and before me, His unworthy minister, renounce the devil and his works?"

Weel, it wad appear that, when he askit that, she gave a girn that fairly frichtit them that saw her, an' they could hear her teeth play dirl thegether in her chafts; but there was naething for it but the ae way or the ither; an' Janet lifted up her hand and renounced the deil before them a'.

"And now," says Mr. Soulis to the guidwives, "home with ye, one and all, and pray to God for His forgiveness."

And he gied Janet his arm, though she had little on her but a sark, and took her up the clachan to her ain door like a leddy of the land, an' her scrieghin' and laughin' as was a scandal to be heard.

There were mony grave folk lang ower their
prayers that nicht; but when the morn cam' there
was sic a fear fell upon a' Ba'weary that the bairns
hid theirsel's, and even the men folk stood and
keekit frae their doors. For there was Janet
comin' doun the clachan,—her or her likeness,
nane could tell,—wi' her neck thrawn, and her
heid on ae side, like a body that has been hangit,
and a girn on her face like an unstreakit corp.
By-an'-by they got used wi' it, and even speered
at her to ken what was wrang; but frae that day
forth she couldnae speak like a Christian woman,
but slavered and played click wi' her teeth like a
pair o' shears; and frae that day forth the name
o' God cam' never on her lips. Whiles she wad try
to say it, but it michtnae be. Them that kenned
best said least; but they never gied that Thing the
name o' Janet M'Clour; for the auld Janet, by
their way o' 't, was in muckle hell that day. But
the minister was neither to haud nor to bind; he
preached about naething but the folk's cruelty that
had gien her a stroke of the palsy; he skelpt the
bairns that meddled her; and he had her up to the
manse that same nicht, and dwalled there a' his lane
wi' her under the Hangin' Shaw.

Weel, time gaed by, and the idler sort com-
menced to think mair lichtly o' that black business. The minister was weel thocht o'; he was
aye late at the writing—folk wad see his can'le doon
by the Dule Water after twal' at e'en ; and he seemed
pleased wi' himsel' and upsitten as at first, though

a' body could see that he was dwining. As for
Janet, she cam' an' she gaed; if she didnae speak
muckle afore, it was reason she should speak less
then; she meddled naebody; but she was an
eldritch thing to see, an' nane wad hae mistrysted
wi' her for Ba'weary glebe.

About the end o' July there cam' a spell o'
weather, the like o' 't never was in that country-
side; it was lown an' het an' heartless; the herds
couldnae win up the Black Hill, the bairns were
ower-weariet to play; an' yet it was gousty too,
wi' claps o' het wund that rummled in the glens,
and bits o' shouers that slockened naething. We
aye thocht it but to thun'er on the morn; but the
morn cam', an' the morn's morning, and it was
aye the same uncanny weather, sair on folks
and bestial. Of a' that were the waur, nane suf-
fered like Mr. Soulis; he could neither sleep nor
eat, he tauld his elders; an' when he wasnae
writin' at his weary book, he wad be stravaguin'
ower a' the country-side like a man possessed,
when a' body else was blithe to keep caller ben
the house.

Abune Hangin' Shaw, in the bield o' the Black
Hill, there 's a bit enclosed grund wi' an iron yett;
and it seems, in the auld days, that was the kirkyaird o' Ba'weary, and consecrated by the papists
before the blessed licht shone upon the kingdom.
It was a great howff, o' Mr. Soulis's onyway; there
he would sit an' consider his sermons; and inded
it 's a bieldy bit. Weel, as he came ower the wast

end o' the Black Hill, ae day, he saw first twa, an'
syne fower, an' syne seeven corbie craws fleein'
round an' round abune the auld kirkyaird. They
flew laigh and heavy, an' squawked to ither as they
gaed; and it was clear to Mr. Soulis that something
had put them frae their ordinar. He wasnae easy
fleyed, an' gaed straucht up to the wa's; and what
suld he find there but a man, or the appearance of
a man, sittin' in the inside upon a grave. He was
of a great stature, an' black as hell, and his een
were singular to see.[1] Mr. Soulis had heard tell
o' black men, mony 's the time; but there was
something unco about this black man that daunted
him. Het as he was, he took a kind o' cauld grue
in the marrow o' his banes; but up he spak' for a'
that; an' says he, " My friend, are you a stranger
in this place? " The black man answered never
a word; he got upon his feet, an' begude to hirsel
to the wa' on the far side; but he aye lookit at the
minister; an' the minister stood an' lookit back;
till a' in a meenute the black man was ower the
wa' an' rinnin' for the bield o' the trees. Mr.
Soulis, he hardly kenned why, ran after him; but
he was sair forjaskit wi' his walk an' the het, un-
halesome weather; and rin as he likit, he got nae
mair than a glisk o' the black man amang the birks,
till he won doun to the foot o' the hillside, an' there

---

[1] It was a common belief in Scotland that the devil ap-
peared as a black man. This appears in several witch-
trials, and, I think, in Law's " Memorials," that delightful
storehouse of the quaint and grisly.

he saw him ance mair, gaun, hap, step, an' lowp, ower Dule Water to the manse.

Mr. Soulis wasnae weel pleased that this fearsome gangrel suld mak' sae free wi' Ba'weary manse; an' he ran the harder, an' wet shoon, ower the burn, an' up the walk; but the deil a black man was there to see. He stepped out upon the road, but there was naebody there; he gaed a' ower the gairden, but na, nae black man. At the hinder end, and a bit feard as was but natural, he lifted the hasp and into the manse; and there was Janet M'Clour before his een, wi' her thrawn craig, and nane sae pleased to see him. And he aye minded sinsyne, when first he set his een upon her, he had the same cauld and deidly grue.

"Janet," says he, "have you seen a black man?"

"A black man?" quo' she. "Save us a'! Ye 're no wise, minister. There 's nae black man in a' Ba'weary."

But she didnae speak plain, ye maun understand; but yam-yammered, like a powny wi' the bit in its moo.

"Weel," says he, "Janet, if there was nae black man, I have spoken with the Accuser of the Brethren."

And he sat down like ane wi' a fever, an' his teeth chittered in his heid.

"Hoots!" says she, "think shame to yoursel', minister," an' gied him a drap brandy that she keept aye by her.

Syne Mr. Soulis gaed into his study amang a'

his books. It 's a lang, laigh, mirk chalmer, per-
ishin' cauld in winter, an' no very dry even in the
top o' the simmer, for the manse stands near the
burn. Sae doun he sat, and thocht of a' that had
come an' gane since he was in Ba'weary, an' his
hame, an' the days when he was a bairn an' ran
daffin' on the braes; and that black man aye ran
in his heid like the owercome of a sang. Aye the
mair he thocht, the mair he thocht o' the black
man. He tried the prayer, an' the words would-
nae come to him; an' he tried, they say, to write
at his book, but he couldnae mak' nae mair o'
that. There was whiles he thocht the black man
was at his oxter, an' the swat stood upon him
cauld as well-water; and there was other whiles
when he cam' to himsel' like a christened bairn and
minded naething.

The upshot was that he gaed to the window an'
stood glowrin' at Dule Water. The trees are unco
thick, an' the water lies deep an' black under the
manse; and there was Janet washin' the cla'es wi'
her coats kilted. She had her back to the minister, an' he, for his pairt, hardly kenned what he
was lookin' at. Syne she turned round, an'
shawed her face; Mr. Soulis had the same cauld
grue as twice that day afore, an' it was borne in
upon him what folk said, that Janet was deid lang
syne, an' this was a bogle in her clay-cauld flesh.
He drew back a pickle and he scanned her nar-
rowly. She was tramp-trampin' in the cla'es,
croonin' to hersel'; and eh! Gude guide us, but

it was a fearsome face. Whiles she sang louder, but there was nae man born o' woman that could tell the words o' her sang; an' whiles she lookit sidelang doun, but there was naething there for her to look at. There gaed a scunner through the flesh upon his banes; and that was Heeven's advertisement. But Mr. Soulis just blamed himsel', he said, to think sae ill of a puir auld afflicted wife that hadnae a freend forby himsel'; an' he put up a bit prayer for him an' her, an' drank a little caller water,—for his heart rose again' the meat,—an' gaed up to his naked bed in the gloaming.

That was a nicht that has never been forgotten in Ba'weary, the nicht o' the seeventeenth of August, seventeen hun'er' an' twal'. It had been het afore, as I hae said, but that nicht it was hetter than ever. The sun gaed doun amang unco-lookin' clouds; it fell as mirk as the pit; no a star, no a breath o' wund; ye couldnae see your han' afore your face, and even the auld folk cuist the covers frae their beds and lay pechin' for their breath. Wi' a' that he had upon his mind, it was gey and unlikely Mr. Soulis wad get muckle sleep. He lay an' he tummled; the gude, caller bed that he got into brunt his very banes; whiles he slept, and whiles he waukened; whiles he heard the time o' nicht, and whiles a tike yowlin' up the muir, as if somebody was deid: whiles he thocht he heard bogles claverin' in his lug, an' whiles he saw spunkies in the room. He behooved, he judged, to be

sick; an' sick he was—little he jaloosed the sick-
ness.

At the hinder end, he got a clearness in his mind,
sat up in his sark on the bedside, and fell thinkin'
ance mair o' the black man an' Janet. He couldnae
weel tell how,—maybe it was the cauld to his feet,
—but it cam' in upon him wi' a spate that there
was some connection between thir twa, an' that
either or baith o' them were bogles. And just at
that moment, in Janet's room, which was neist to
his, there cam' a stramp o' feet as if men were
wars'lin', an' then a loud bang; an' then a wund
gaed reishling round the fower quarters of the
house; an' then a' was ance mair as seelent as the
grave.

Mr. Soulis was feard for neither man nor deevil.
He got his tinder-box, an' lit a can'le, an' made
three steps o' 't ower to Janet's door. It was on
the hasp, an' he pushed it open, an' keeked bauldly
in. It was a big room, as big as the minister's ain,
an' plenished wi' grand, auld, solid gear, for he had
naething else. There was a fower-posted bed wi'
auld tapestry; and a braw cabinet of aik, that was
fu' o' the minister's divinity books, an' put there
to be out o' the gate; an' a wheen duds o' Janet's
lying here and there about the floor   But nae
Janet could Mr. Soulis see, nor ony sign of a
contention. In he gaed (an' there 's few that wad
hae followed him), an' lookit a' round, an' listened.
But there was naethin' to be heard neither inside
the manse nor in a' Ba'weary parish, an' naethin'

to be seen but the muckle shadows turnin' round the can'le. An' then a' at aince the minister's heart played dunt an' stood stock-still, an' a cauld wund blew amang the hairs o' his heid. Whaten a weary sicht was that for the puir man's een! For there was Janet hangin' frae a nail beside the auld aik cabinet; her heid aye lay on her shouther, her een were steeked, the tongue projeckit frae her mouth, and her heels were twa feet clear abune the floor.

"God forgive us all!" thocht Mr. Soulis, "poor Janet 's dead."

He cam' a step nearer to the corp; an' then his heart fair whammled in his inside. For—by what cantrip it wad ill beseem a man to judge—she was hingin' frae a single nail an' by a single wursted thread for darnin' hose.

It 's an awfu' thing to be your lane at nicht wi' siccan prodigies o' darkness; but Mr. Soulis was strong in the Lord. He turned an' gaed his ways oot o' that room, and lockit the door ahint him; and step by step doon the stairs, as heavy as leed; and set doon the can'le on the table at the stair-foot. He couldnae pray, he couldnae think, he was dreepin' wi' caul' swat, an' naething could he hear but the dunt-dunt-duntin' o' his ain heart. He micht maybe have stood there an hour, or maybe twa, he minded sae little; when a' o' a sudden he heard a laigh, uncanny steer upstairs; a foot gaed to an' fro in the cham'er whaur the corp was hingin'; syne the door was opened,

though he minded weel that he had lockit it; an'
syne there was a step upon the landin', an' it
seemed to him as if the corp was lookin' ower the
rail and doun upon him whaur he stood.

He took up the can'le again (for he couldnae
want the licht), and, as saftly as ever he could,
gaed straucht out o' the manse an' to the far end
o' the causeway. It was aye pit-mirk; the flame
o' the can'le, when he set it on the grund, brunt
steedy and clear as in a room; naething moved,
but the Dule Water seepin' and sabbin' doon the
glen, an' yon unhaly footstep that cam' ploddin'
doun the stairs inside the manse. He kenned the
foot ower-weel, for it was Janet's; and at ilka step
that cam' a wee thing nearer, the cauld got deeper
in his vitals. He commended his soul to Him
that made an' keepit him; "and, O Lord," said
he, "give me strength this night to war against
the powers of evil."

By this time the foot was comin' through the
passage for the door; he could hear a hand skirt
alang the wa', as if the fearsome thing was feelin'
for its way. The saughs tossed an' maned thegether,
a long sigh cam' ower the hills, the flame o' the
can'le was blawn aboot; an' there stood the corp
of Thrawn Janet, wi' her grogram goun an' her
black mutch, wi' the heid aye upon the shouther,
an' the girn still upon the face o' 't,—leevin', ye wad
hae said—deid, as Mr. Soulis weel kenned,—upon
the threshold o' the manse.

It 's a strange thing that the saul of man should

be that thirled into his perishable body; but the minister saw that, an' his heart didnae break.

She didnae stand there lang; she began to move again, an' cam' slowly toward Mr. Soulis whaur he stood under the saughs. A' the life o' his body, a' the strength o' his speerit, were glowerin' frae his een. It seemed she was gaun to speak, but wanted words, an' made a sign wi' the left hand. There cam' a clap o' wund, like a cat's fuff; oot gaed the can'le, the saughs skrieghed like folk; an' Mr. Soulis kenned that, live or die, this was the end o' 't.

"Witch, beldam, devil!" he cried, "I charge you, by the power of God, begone—if you be dead, to the grave; if you be damned, to hell."

An' at that moment the Lord's ain hand out o' the heevens struck the Horror whaur it stood; the auld, deid, desecrated corp o' the witch-wife, sae lang keepit frae the grave and hirselled round by deils, lowed up like a brunstane spunk and fell in ashes to the grund; the thunder followed, peal on dirling peal, the rairing rain upon the back o' that; and Mr. Soulis lowped through the garden hedge, and ran, wi' skelloch upon skelloch, for the clachan.

That same mornin' John Christie saw the black man pass the Muckle Cairn as it was chappin' six; before eicht, he gaed by the change-house at Knockdow; an' no lang after, Sandy M'Lellan saw him gaun linkin' doun the braes frae Kilmackerlie. There 's little doubt but it was him that

dwalled sae lang in Janet's body; but he was awa'
at last; and sinsyne the deil has never fashed us
in Ba'weary.

But it was a sair dispensation for the minister;
lang, lang he lay ravin' in his bed; and frae that
hour to this, he was the man ye ken the day.

This is the end of this publication.

Any remaining blank pages are for our book binding requirements and are blank on purpose.

To search thousands of interesting publications like this one, please remember to visit our website at:

http://www.kessinger.net